MATH Trailblazers®

A BALANCED MATHEMATICS PROGRAM INTEGRATING SCIENCE AND LANGUAGE ARTS

Unit Resource Guide
Unit 16
Collecting and Organizing Data

THIRD EDITION

KENDALL/HUNT PUBLISHING COMPANY
4050 Westmark Drive   Dubuque, Iowa 52002

A TIMS® Curriculum
University of Illinois at Chicago

UIC The University of Illinois
at Chicago

The original edition was based on work supported by the National Science Foundation under grant No. MDR 9050226 and the University of Illinois at Chicago. Any opinions, findings, and conclusions or recommendations expressed in this publication are those of the author(s) and do not necessarily reflect the views of the granting agencies.

Letter Home

Collecting and Organizing Data

Date: _____

Dear Family Member:

The United States Department of Agriculture (USDA) has published guidelines for sound eating habits as shown in the model called My Pyramid. This unit features a lab in which your child uses the classification system shown in the pyramid to sort into six groups, foods he or she has eaten during one day. Your child will analyze the data to evaluate whether or not he or she has made healthy food choices. To set the stage for the lab, your child will read a story about Martians who collect data about the diets of Earthling children to find out why they are so full of energy.

My pyramid

As we survey food choices and practice collecting and organizing data at school, you can provide additional support at home by doing some of the following activities:

- **Favorite Foods List.** Write a list of your ten favorite foods, and ask your child to classify them according to the six categories shown in the pyramid. Then, invite your child to draw conclusions about the nutritional value of the foods you listed.

- **Sorting Groceries.** After your next trip to the supermarket, invite your child to sort some of the groceries according to the categories in the pyramid.

Thank you for your continued interest in your child's mathematics development.

Sincerely,

_____

Carta al Hogar

Fecha: _____

Estimado miembro de familia:

El Departamento de Agricultura de los Estados Unidos (USDA) ha publicado guías para buenos hábitos alimenticios como se muestra en el modelo llamado Mi Pirámide. Esta unidad presenta una investigación en la cuál su hijo/a usa el sistema de clasificación que se muestra en la pirámide para clasificar en los seis grupos la comida que ha comido durante un día. Su hijo/a analizará los datos para ver si ha tomado decisiones alimenticias saludables. Como preparación para esta investigación, su hijo/a leerá una historia acerca de unos marcianos que recogen datos acerca de la comida que comen los niños de la tierra para averiguar porqué tienen tanta energía.

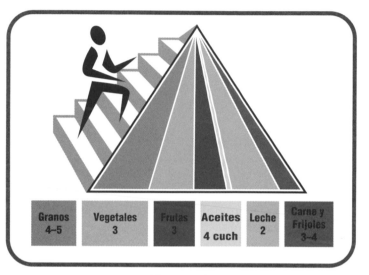

Mi pirámide

Mientras hacemos este estudio sobre las opciones alimentarias y practicamos cómo reunir y organizar información en la escuela, usted puede dar su apoyo adicional en casa haciendo algunas de las siguientes actividades:

- **Lista de alimentos favoritos.** Escriba la lista de sus diez alimentos favoritos, y pídale a su hijo/a que los clasifique de acuerdo con las seis categorías que se muestran en la pirámide. Luego invite a su hijo/a a que saque conclusiones acerca del valor nutricional de los alimentos de la lista.
- **Clasificación de los alimentos comprados.** Al volver del supermercado, invite a su hijo/a a que clasifique algunos de los alimentos según las categorías de la pirámide.

Gracias por su continuo interés en el desarrollo de las habilidades matemáticas de su hijo/a.

Atentamente,

_____

Table of Contents

Unit 16
Collecting and Organizing Data

Unit 16

Outline
Collecting and Organizing Data

Unit Summary

Estimated Class Sessions

5

Offered as an opportunity for teacher-guided assessment, this unit encourages students to work more independently on data collection and analysis. Students review and discuss the TIMS Laboratory Method with *The Martians* Adventure Book before beginning the *Healthy Kids* Lab. Students collect and organize data about their daily eating habits to see if it falls in a range. The DPP includes items that provide practice and assessment of students' use of math facts strategies, including using a ten.

Major Concept Focus

- using a survey to study variables
- classification
- comparing two sets of data
- TIMS Laboratory Method
- *Adventure Book:* TIMS Laboratory Method

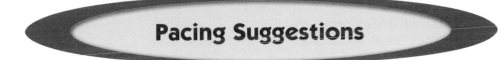

Pacing Suggestions

Utilize *Math Trailblazers®* connections to other subjects:

- Read and discuss the Adventure Book story in Lesson 1 *The Martians* during language arts.
- Lesson 3 *Healthy Kids* is a laboratory investigation. Compare and discuss students' data during science time.
- This unit can complement a science unit on nutrition.

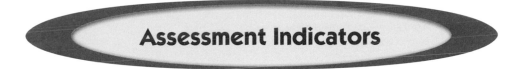

Assessment Indicators

Use the following Assessment Indicators and the *Observational Assessment Record* that follows the Background section in this unit to assess students on key ideas.

A1. Can students collect and organize data in a table?

A2. Can students make and interpret bar graphs?

A3. Can students use data to solve problems?

A4. Do students use math facts strategies to add (direct modeling, counting strategies, or reasoning from known facts)?

Unit Planner

KEY: SG = Student Guide, AB = Adventure Book, URG = Unit Resource Guide, DPP = Daily Practice and Problems, and TIG = Teacher Implementation Guide.

	Lesson Information	Supplies	Copies/Transparencies

Lesson 1
The Martians

URG Pages 18–24
SG Page 331
AB Pages 69–76

DPP A–B

Estimated Class Sessions

1

Adventure Book
A group of Martians decides to travel to Earth and study Earthlings. They land near a school. Curious about the source of the children's energy, the Martians decide to study what the children eat. This Adventure Book provides the setting for the lab *Healthy Kids* in Lesson 3.

Math Facts Strategies
Assign DPP items A and B. Item A provides practice with grouping and counting beans by twos, fives, and tens and counting leftovers. Item B is a story problem *Gold Pieces* from the *Student Guide* in which students practice counting on and counting back.

Homework
The *Favorite Foods* Homework Page, which asks children to list ten of their favorite foods, must be completed before beginning the next lesson *Food Sort*.

Lesson 2
Food Sort

URG Pages 25–32
SG Pages 333–335

DPP C–D

Estimated Class Sessions

1

Activity
This activity prepares students for the data collection in the lab *Healthy Kids* in the following lesson. Children become familiar with food groups by sorting ten of their favorite foods into six food groups. Then children classify fruits and vegetables.

Math Facts Strategies
DPP item C provides practice with addition math facts. Item D is a story problem from the *Student Guide.*

Homework
Students complete the *Joni's and Bobbie's Breakfasts* Homework Page.

Assessment
Use Assessment Indicator A1 and the *Observational Assessment Record* to document students' abilities to collect and organize data.

Supplies:
• *Eating the Alphabet: Fruits and Vegetables from A to Z* by Lois Ehlert, optional

Copies/Transparencies:
• 1 copy of *Observational Assessment Record* URG Pages 9–10 to be used throughout this unit

---

Lesson 3
Healthy Kids

URG Pages 33–45
SG Pages 337–345

DPP E–J

Estimated Class Sessions

3

Lab
In this teacher-guided lab, students collect data on what they eat for one day and compare their diets to suggested food group amounts. Students then analyze their personal data to see if they need to make changes to achieve a healthy diet.

Math Facts Strategies
DPP items E, G, and I provide math facts practice. Item F is a problem from the *Student Guide.* Items H and J ask students to group and count objects by twos, fives, and tens.

Homework
Students collect their data for the lab and record it on the *I Ate That!* Homework Pages.

Supplies:
• 1 cup of cereal, optional

Copies/Transparencies:
• 1 transparency of Servings data table SG Page 338
• 1 transparency of *My Pyramid* URG Page 42 or classroom poster of food groups and recommended servings
• 1 copy of *Individual Assessment Record Sheet* TIG Assessment section per student, previously copied for use throughout the year

	Lesson Information	Supplies	Copies/ Transparencies
	Assessment 1. Students complete the *David's and Cindy's Food* Assessment Pages. Use Assessment Indicators A2 and A3 and the *Observational Assessment Record* to note whether students can make and interpret bar graphs and use data to solve problems. 2. Use Assessment Indicator A4 and the *Observational Assessment Record* to document students' progress with the math facts in Group F. Note students' strategies. 3. Transfer appropriate assessment documentation from the Unit 16 *Observational Assessment Record* to students' *Individual Assessment Record Sheets*.		

Preparing for Upcoming Lessons

In Unit 17 students will need egg cartons to group objects. Encourage students to bring in egg cartons from home.

Connections

A current list of literature and software connections is available at *www.mathtrailblazers.com*. You can also find information on connections in the *Teacher Implementation Guide* Literature List and Software List sections.

Literature Connections
Suggested Titles
* Ehlert, Lois. *Eating the Alphabet: Fruits and Vegetables from A to Z.* Econo-Clad Books, Topeka, KS, 1999. (Lesson 2)

Software Connections
* *Kid Pix* helps students draw, write, and illustrate math concepts.
* *Math Concepts One . . . Two . . . Three!* provides practice sorting objects and making simple bar graphs.
* *Mighty Math Carnival Countdown* provides practice sorting sets by attributes including sorting numbers by size, more or less, and even or odd.
* *Sunbuddy Math Playhouse* asks students to sort musical instruments by an increasing number of attributes.
* *Thinkin' Things Collection I: Toony the Loon's Lagoon* asks students to identify various attributes of the characters and to observe a row of birds with various attributes and build the next bird in line.

Teaching All Math Trailblazers Students

Math Trailblazers lessons are designed for students with a wide range of abilities. The lessons are flexible and do not require significant adaptation for diverse learning styles or academic levels. However, when needed, lessons can be tailored to allow students to engage their abilities to the greatest extent possible while building knowledge and skills.

To assist you in meeting the needs of all students in your classroom, this section contains information about some of the features in the curriculum that allow all students access to mathematics. For additional information, see the Teaching the *Math Trailblazers* Student: Meeting Individual Needs section in the *Teacher Implementation Guide*.

Differentiation Opportunities in this Unit

Laboratory Experiments

Laboratory experiments enable students to solve problems using a variety of representations including pictures, tables, graphs, and symbols. Teachers can assign or adapt parts of the analysis according to the student's ability. The following lesson is a lab:

- Lesson 3 *Healthy Kids*

Unit 16

Background
Collecting and Organizing Data

TIMS Laboratory Method

The survey in this unit gives students an opportunity to practice using the TIMS Laboratory Method in the context of studying healthy food choices. Students have repeatedly used the TIMS Laboratory Method as a tool for finding answers to their own questions. The four steps of the TIMS Laboratory Method are addressed in an *Adventure Book* and in a lab. Their use in the *Adventure Book* reinforces the idea that the laboratory method provides powerful tools for students to use in everyday life to solve many kinds of problems.

This unit begins with the Adventure Book *The Martians,* which poses the lab question: What do children eat? Encourage students to decide how to use each of the four laboratory steps to answer the Martians' question. Lesson 2 *Food Sort* provides students with experience in categorizing food items into food groups. These lessons culminate in the lab *Healthy Kids* in Lesson 3, in which students investigate what they eat over the course of one day. They then compare their diets to government guidelines.

The lab in this unit can be used to assess students' progress toward independent use of the tools in the TIMS Laboratory Method. Observe students as they work through the lab. Specifically, check to see that students:

- Draw a picture with defined variables.
- Collect data and organize it in an appropriately labeled data table.
- Organize and plot data in a graph that has an appropriate title and correctly labeled and scaled axes.
- Accurately interpret the results.

For further information on the TIMS Laboratory Method, refer to the TIMS Tutor: *The TIMS Laboratory Method* in the *Teacher Implementation Guide.* You might want to place this lab in students' portfolios. For further information on portfolios, refer to the TIMS Tutor: *Portfolios* in the *Teacher Implementation Guide.*

Diet

Food availability and cultural diversity are two issues that may need to be carefully addressed in some classrooms. First, the foods students eat are usually controlled by adult family members rather than the children. In some families, healthy food choices may be limited or lacking. Therefore, we ask each child to analyze his or her own diet without making comparisons with the diets of their classmates. The *David's and Cindy's Food* Assessment Pages, in which children think and write about the diets of two imaginary people, allow students to make this type of comparison. Second, some students may need guidance in respecting the diets of children who eat soup or rice and vegetables for a healthy breakfast instead of a popular cereal.

Resources

- United States Department of Agriculture. *Dietary Guidelines for Americans 2005.* Washington DC, 2005.
- Food Guide Pyramid Information can be accessed on the internet at http:www.mypyramid.gov.

Observational Assessment Record

(A1) Can students collect and organize data in a table?

(A2) Can students make and interpret bar graphs?

(A3) Can students use data to solve problems?

(A4) Do students use math facts strategies to add (direct modeling, counting strategies, or reasoning from known facts)?

(A5) _____

Name	A1	A2	A3	A4	A5	Comments
1.						
2.						
3.						
4.						
5.						
6.						
7.						
8.						
9.						
10.						
11.						
12.						
13.						

Name	A1	A2	A3	A4	A5	Comments
14.						
15.						
16.						
17.						
18.						
19.						
20.						
21.						
22.						
23.						
24.						
25.						
26.						
27.						
28.						
29.						
30.						
31.						
32.						

Unit 16

Daily Practice and Problems
Collecting and Organizing Data

A DPP Menu for Unit 16

Two Daily Practice and Problems (DPP) items are included for each class session listed in the Unit Outline. A scope and sequence chart for the DPP is in the *Teacher Implementation Guide*.

Icons in the Teacher Notes column designate the subject matter of each DPP item. Each item falls into one or more of the categories listed below. A menu of the DPP items for Unit 16 follows.

Ⓝ **Number Sense** A, F, H, J	▨ **Computation** B, D, F	⧗ **Time**	⬗ **Geometry**
⁷₊₃ **Math Facts Strategies** C, E, G, I	$ **Money**	▰ **Measurement**	◩ **Data**

Addition Math Facts

In this unit, students practice the addition facts for Group F (9 + 1, 9 + 2, 9 + 3, 9 + 4, 10 + 1, 10 + 2, 10 + 3, and 10 + 4). Facts in Group F can be solved by counting on and using ten. See DPP items C, E, G, and I for practice with these facts. Item I can also assess the facts in Group F. Use Assessment Indicator A4 and the *Observational Assessment Record* to document students' progress with these facts.

For more information about the distribution and assessment of math facts, see the DPP Guide in Unit 11 and the TIMS Tutor: *Math Facts* in the *Teacher Implementation Guide*.

Problem–Solving Story: *The Boy Who Traveled to Find a Hard Problem II*

DPP items B, D, and F refer to the story *The Boy Who Traveled to Find a Hard Problem II*. The story precedes the first lesson in the *Student Guide* and provides a context for addition and subtraction problems. Students write their solutions in their *Student Guides*.

 **Daily Practice and Problems**

Students may solve the items individually, in groups, or as a class. The items may also be assigned for homework. The DPPs are also available on the Teacher Resource CD.

Student Questions	Teacher Notes

A Grouping Beans

N

1. Group the beans by twos and then fill in the blanks for this statement:

   _____ groups of _____ and _____ left over.

2. Now group them by fives and fill in the blanks again.

   _____ groups of _____ and _____ left over.

3. Now group them by tens and fill in the blanks again.

   _____ groups of _____ and _____ left over.

Put some beans (less than 50) on the overhead and have children take turns grouping them by twos, fives, and tens, each time recording the work on the blank lines. Answers will vary depending on the number of beans used. This activity will be repeated in items H and J, so keep track of the number of beans used each time to prevent repeating numbers.

B More from *The Boy Who Traveled to Find a Hard Problem*

Turn to page 328 in your *Student Guide.* We are going to read another page in our story about the boy who liked to solve hard problems.

Go to *Student Guide* page 328 and read *Gold Pieces* to the children. Encourage students to use tools such as manipulatives or *100 Charts.* When several children have shared their solutions, show the class this solution. Say, *"The boy instructed the king to count by tens from 39. The boy said, '49, 59. That makes 20. Since you only need 57 gold pieces, count back two from 20. You need 18 more gold pieces.'"* Model the boy's solution using manipulatives, a drawing, or a *100 Chart.*

Student Questions	Teacher Notes

C **Making and Using Ten**

A. $9 + 1 =$

B. $9 + 2 =$

C. $9 + 3 =$

D. $9 + 4 =$

Encourage students to share any patterns they see in the problems. Students might solve the problems by making ten. For example, $9 + 4$ can be thought of as $10 + 3$.

A. 10   B. 11

C. 12   D. 13

D *Royal Rabbits*

Turn to page 329 in your *Student Guide.* We are going to read another page in our story about the boy who liked to solve hard problems.

Read the *Royal Rabbits* page aloud, *Student Guide* page 329, and have students solve the problem. Allow children to use the tools available to them and to share their solutions. Then, explain this solution. Say, *"The boy said, 'Just count backwards 15 rabbits by fives, starting at 55—50, 45, 40. You see, 40 old rabbits plus 15 new ones make 55 altogether.' The king was overjoyed to have answers to both his hard problems. He gave the boy a golden bird."* Model the boy's solution using manipulatives, a drawing, or a *100 Chart.*

Student Questions	Teacher Notes

E **Related Math Facts**

What other number sentences relate to these four number sentences?

1. $10 + 1 = 11$

2. $10 + 3 = 13$

3. $100 + 10 = 110$

4. $30 + 100 = 130$

1. $1 + 10 = 11$
   $11 - 1 = 10$
   $11 - 10 = 1$

2. $3 + 10 = 13$
   $13 - 3 = 10$
   $13 - 10 = 3$

3. $10 + 100 = 110$
   $110 - 10 = 100$
   $110 - 100 = 10$

4. $100 + 30 = 130$
   $130 - 100 = 30$
   $130 - 30 = 100$

F *Home Again*

Turn to page 330 in your *Student Guide*. We are going to read the last page in our story about the boy who liked to solve hard problems.

Find *Home Again, Student Guide* page 330, and remind students that the boy was rewarded with a goose that lays golden eggs for solving the king's hard problem. Read the story's ending to the children. Challenge children to make up their own problems concerning the bird and the golden eggs. Allow a few children to share their problems with the class now, and use other problems as time permits.

Student Questions	Teacher Notes

G **Math Facts 1**

1. 9 + 1 =   1 + 9 =

2. 2 + 10 =   10 + 2 =

3. 3 + 9 =   9 + 3 =

4. 4 + 10 =   10 + 4 =

Have students tell how the two problems in each question are alike. They should notice that the order of the addends does not change the sum. We call these turn-around facts.

1. 10   10
2. 12   12
3. 12   12
4. 14   14

H **More Grouping Beans**

1. Group the beans by twos and then fill in the blanks for this statement:

   _____ groups of _____ and _____ left over.

2. Now group them by fives and fill in the blanks again.

   _____ groups of _____ and _____ left over.

3. Now group them by tens and fill in the blanks again.

   _____ groups of _____ and _____ left over.

Put a different number of beans (less than 50) on the overhead and have students take turns grouping them by twos, fives, and tens, each time recording the work on the blank lines. Answers will vary depending on the number of beans used. This activity will be repeated in item J so keep track of the number of beans used each time to prevent repeating numbers.

1 Math Facts 2

1. $9 + 1 =$

2. $10 + 4 =$

3. $9 + 2 =$

4. $10 + 1 =$

5. $9 + 4 =$

6. $10 + 2 =$

7. $3 + 10 =$

8. $3 + 9 =$

Explain your strategy for Question 8.

1. 10
2. 14
3. 11
4. 11
5. 13
6. 12
7. 13
8. 12

Strategies will vary. Possible responses: $3 + 9$ is the same as $2 + 10$ or 12. Or, count on 3 from 9: 10, 11, 12.

J Even More Grouping Beans

1. Group the beans by twos and then fill in the blanks for this statement:

   _____ groups of _____ and _____ left over.

Put a different number of beans (less than 50) on the overhead and have children take turns grouping them by twos, fives, and tens, each time recording the work on the blank lines. Answers will vary depending on the number of beans used.

2. Now group them by fives and fill in the blanks again.

   _____ groups of _____ and _____ left over.

3. Now group them by tens and fill in the blanks again.

   _____ groups of _____ and _____ left over.

Lesson 1

The Martians

Lesson Overview

A group of Martians decides to travel to Earth and study Earthlings. They land near a school and notice the energy of the children there. Curious about the source of the children's energy, the Martians decide to study what children eat. This Adventure Book story provides the setting for Lesson 3 *Healthy Kids,* a lab in which children collect data on the kinds of foods and the number of servings they eat in one day.

Key Content

- Collecting and organizing data for a survey.
- Reviewing the TIMS Laboratory Method.

Math Facts Strategies

Assign DPP items A and B. Item A provides practice grouping and counting beans by twos, fives, and tens and counting leftovers. Item B is a story problem *Gold Pieces* from the *Student Guide* in which students practice counting on and counting back.

Homework

The *Favorite Foods* Homework Page, which asks children to list ten of their favorite foods, must be completed before beginning the next lesson *Food Sort.*

Curriculum Sequence

Before This Unit

The TIMS Laboratory Method

Students used the TIMS Laboratory Method to investigate weather in Units 2 and 11. They also used it in other laboratory investigations in Units 5, 6, 9, and 14.

Materials List

Supplies and Copies

Student	Teacher
Supplies for Each Student	**Supplies**
Copies	**Copies/Transparencies**

All blackline masters including assessment, transparency, and DPP masters are also on the Teacher Resource CD.

Student Books

The Boy Who Traveled to Find a Hard Problem II Gold Pieces (*Student Guide* Page 328)
Favorite Foods (*Student Guide* Page 331)
The Martians (*Adventure Book* Pages 69–76)

Daily Practice and Problems

DPP items A–B (*Unit Resource Guide* Page 12)

Suggestions for using the DPPs are on page 24.

A. Grouping Beans (URG p. 12)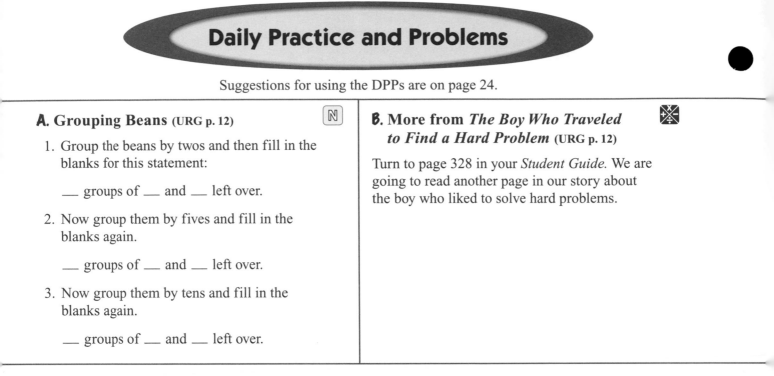

1. Group the beans by twos and then fill in the blanks for this statement:

   __ groups of __ and __ left over.

2. Now group them by fives and fill in the blanks again.

   __ groups of __ and __ left over.

3. Now group them by tens and fill in the blanks again.

   __ groups of __ and __ left over.

B. More from *The Boy Who Traveled to Find a Hard Problem* (URG p. 12)

Turn to page 328 in your *Student Guide.* We are going to read another page in our story about the boy who liked to solve hard problems.

Teaching the Activity

Read *The Martians* Adventure Book to launch a discussion about setting up a survey about what students eat. Then, ask students to think of ways to tell a scientist about the kinds and amounts of foods that children in this class eat. Invite them to discuss how to organize this information. Discuss the TIMS Laboratory Method as a useful way to collect and analyze the data. As the unit progresses, students should think about and discuss (with teacher guidance) why each step of the TIMS Laboratory Method is important in conducting a survey. In the TIMS Laboratory Method:

1. A **picture** helps organize and communicate what we are going to do.

2. A **data table** organizes the data collection.

3. A **graph** displays the data in a way that makes it easier to see patterns.

4. **Data analysis** helps us understand what information we can get from the data collected.

The following discussion prompts develop a discussion about how the TIMS Laboratory Method can be used to study the kinds of food students eat.

Discussion Prompts

Page 70

*   *What do you think the Martians might want to study about Earthlings?*

The Martians

On the planet Mars...

"I need volunteers for a mission to Earth," announced the famous Martian scientist named Brainy. "We must study Earthlings! Who wants to go?"

70   AB · Grade 1 · Unit 16 · Lesson 1

Adventure Book - page 70

As soon as the Martians landed, they saw an interesting looking building. Many small Earthlings were in and around it. Some were sitting at desks, reading and talking together. Others were playing outside, running and jumping. They were so busy!

Dopp and Zorka looked at the Earthlings and wondered where they got all that energy! They wondered what the Earthlings ate to keep their bodies going. They agreed that this would be a good thing to study.

AB • Grade 1 • Unit 16 • Lesson 1 73

Adventure Book - page 73

Discussion Prompts

Page 73

- *What are the Martians planning to study?*

The types of foods Earthlings eat.

- *What are some things that the Martians might study?*

Types of food and amount of each food eaten; healthy or unhealthy food.

- *Do we all eat the same type of food everyday? What kinds of foods do we eat?*

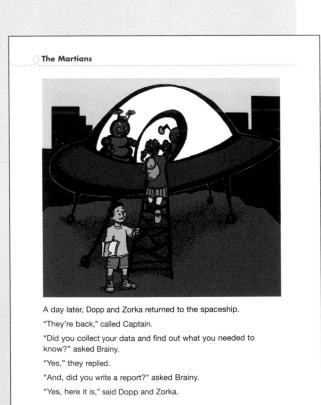

A day later, Dopp and Zorka returned to the spaceship.

"They're back," called Captain.

"Did you collect your data and find out what you needed to know?" asked Brainy.

"Yes," they replied.

"And, did you write a report?" asked Brainy.

"Yes, here it is," said Dopp and Zorka.

74 AB • Grade 1 • Unit 16 • Lesson 1

Adventure Book - page 74

Page 74

- *How might the Martians collect their data about what Earthlings eat? Sketch a data table and label the columns to show how you think they might collect their data.*

Students' data tables will vary depending upon what they think the variables are. Some students may label the columns of their data tables as "Type of Food" and "Healthy or Unhealthy" while others may label them as "Type of Food" and "Amount Eaten." Encourage students to discuss their ideas.

- *How might the Martians organize their data in their report? How might they label the axes on their graph?*

The organization of data and the labels in the graph will vary depending upon the variables students think the Martians might study.

Page 75

- *What kinds of foods might the healthy kids eat? Which of these healthy foods do you like?*

Discussing students' favorites will help prepare them for their homework assignment.

- *What kinds of unhealthy foods might kids eat? Which of these unhealthy foods do you like?*

Encouraging students to tell their favorite unhealthy foods will prepare them for their homework assignment. (Unhealthy foods have little or no nutritional value as described by the USDA Food Pyramid.)

The Martians

"We found out that some Earthlings have lots of energy and others do not," said Dopp.

"Earthlings eat a lot of different foods," said Zorka.

"It seems that the Earthlings who ate certain kinds of food were healthy and had lots of energy," said Dopp.

"Yeah, but some Earthlings ate other kinds of food and they were tired and seemed unhealthy," said Zorka.

AB • Grade 1 • Unit 16 • Lesson 1   **75**

Adventure Book - page 75

Page 76

- *How might the Martians find out why some Earthlings eat unhealthy foods?*

They can conduct a survey and ask questions of a group of Earthlings.

The Martians

"Why would they eat food that would make them tired and unhealthy?" asked Brainy.

"We didn't find out," said Dopp.

"But next time we go to Earth, we're going to find out!" said Zorka.

76 AB • Grade 1 • Unit 16 • Lesson 1

Adventure Book - page 76

Favorite Foods

Homework

Dear Family Member:

Please help your child record his or her favorite foods in preparation for conducting a food survey.

Thank you for your help.

List ten of your favorite foods.

1. _____
2. _____
3. _____
4. _____ 
5. _____
6. _____
7. _____
8. _____
9. _____
10. _____

The Martians   SG • Grade 1 • Unit 16 • Lesson 1   331

Student Guide - page 331

Homework and Practice

- The *Favorite Foods* Homework Page, which asks children to list ten of their favorite foods, must be completed before beginning the next lesson *Food Sort*.

- Assign DPP items A and B. Item A provides practice grouping and counting beans by twos, fives, and tens and counting leftovers. Item B is a story problem *Gold Pieces* from the *Student Guide* in which students practice counting on and counting back.

Lesson 2

Food Sort

Lesson Overview

Estimated Class Sessions

1

This activity prepares students for the data collection in Lesson 3, the *Healthy Kids* lab. Children become familiar with food groups by sorting ten of their favorite foods into food groups, a classification system suggested by the U.S. Department of Agriculture. Then children participate in classifying fruits and vegetables.

Key Content
- Collecting and organizing data.
- Classifying items into categories.

Key Vocabulary
- food group
- values
- variables

Math Facts Strategies

DPP item C provides addition math facts practice. Item D is a story problem from the *Student Guide*.

Homework

Students complete the *Joni's and Bobbie's Breakfasts* Homework Page.

Assessment

Use Assessment Indicator A1 and the *Observational Assessment Record* to document students' abilities to collect and organize data.

Materials List

Supplies and Copies

Student	Teacher
Supplies for Each Student	**Supplies** • *Eating the Alphabet: Fruits and Vegetables from A to Z* by Lois Ehlert, optional
Copies	**Copies/Transparencies** • 1 copy of *Observational Assessment Record* to be used throughout this unit (*Unit Resource Guide* Pages 9–10)

All blackline masters including assessment, transparency, and DPP masters are also on the Teacher Resource CD.

Student Books

Royal Rabbits (*Student Guide* Page 329)
Favorite Foods (*Student Guide* Page 331 from Lesson 1)
Food Group Sort 1 (*Student Guide* Page 333)
Food Group Sort 2 (*Student Guide* Page 334)
Joni's and Bobbie's Breakfasts (*Student Guide* Page 335)

Daily Practice and Problems

DPP items C–D (*Unit Resource Guide* Page 13)

Assessment Tools

Observational Assessment Record (*Unit Resource Guide* Pages 9–10)

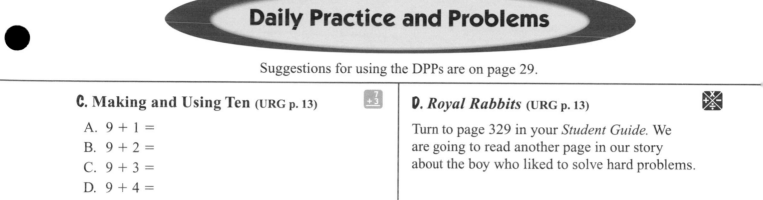

C. Making and Using Ten (URG p. 13)

A. $9 + 1 =$

B. $9 + 2 =$

C. $9 + 3 =$

D. $9 + 4 =$

D. *Royal Rabbits* (URG p. 13)

Turn to page 329 in your *Student Guide.* We are going to read another page in our story about the boy who liked to solve hard problems.

Before the Activity

Children need to complete the *Favorite Foods* Homework Page from Lesson 1 before they can proceed with this activity.

Complete this activity before the next lesson, the *Healthy Kids* Lab, so that children understand how to classify food items into food groups. Your students' performance on the *Joni's and Bobbie's Breakfasts* Homework Page can help you determine whether they need more practice before proceeding to the lab.

Teaching the Activity

Using the completed *Favorite Foods* Homework Page from Lesson 1, students work with a partner to decide where each of their favorite foods should be placed on the *Food Group Sort 1* Activity Page. Spend some time discussing the different groups. We suggest, however, that the bulk of the discussion occur after students have spent some time trying to classify their favorite foods.

After students complete this warm-up activity, invite them to explore ways to classify fruits and vegetables. The book *Eating the Alphabet: Fruits and Vegetables from A to Z* by Lois Ehlert is an excellent resource for exploring a variety of fruits and vegetables. You can start either by going through the book and discussing the classifications or by soliciting examples of fruits and vegetables from the children and using the book to find additional examples. Either way, use a table to help children record their classifications, as in Figure 1.

During the discussion, guide children to see that sometimes putting foods into groups can be tricky since it is not always obvious what category an item belongs in. Lois Ehlert's book presents 35 fruits, 29 vegetables, and 11 foods that she classifies as fruits/vegetables. These foods can be classified in either culinary or botanical terms. For this sorting task, you can focus on the everyday (culinary) usage of the foods. For example, a tomato is most often classified in everyday terms as a vegetable. However, a botanist would classify a tomato as a fruit. If you classify the foods keeping their everyday use in mind, there are 36 fruits and 39 vegetables in Ehlert's book.

Student Guide - page 333 *(Answers on p. 31)*

Fruits	Vegetables
apple	corn
pear	peas
orange	potato
kiwi	broccoli
strawberry	tomato

Figure 1: *A table showing the classification of fruits and vegetables*

Have student pairs work on the *Food Group Sort 2* Activity Page for additional practice in classifying foods. Some of the foods can fall into more than one food group. For example, a peanut butter sandwich belongs to both the bread (1) and meat (5) groups. A hamburger can belong to the meat group alone (the patty) or to the meat, bread, and vegetable groups (the patty, the bun, and onion, pickle, and lettuce) depending on how each person thinks of a hamburger.

Math Facts Strategies

DPP item C explores using ten to derive addition math facts.

Homework and Practice

- The *Joni's and Bobbie's Breakfasts* Homework Page provides more experience with classification into food groups. Several of the items can be classified in more than one group (e.g., bacon can be in the meat and fat groups). Discussion of these items will reinforce the previous activities in this lesson.

Joni's Breakfast	Bobbie's Breakfast
rice puffs 1	waffle 1, 6
milk 4	strawberries 3
slices of apples 3	whipped cream 6
banana bread 1, 3	maple syrup 6
orange juice 3	bacon 5, 6
	milk 4

- Assign DPP item D that is a story problem *Royal Rabbits* from the *Student Guide*.

Assessment

Use the *Observational Assessment Record* to document students' abilities to collect and organize data.

Literature Connection

Ehlert, Lois. *Eating the Alphabet: Fruits and Vegetables from A to Z.* Econo-Clad Books, Topeka, KS, 1999.

Name _____ Date _____

Food Group Sort 2

Sort the foods below into these six food groups. Write the number of the group after each food. Some foods are in more than one group.

Food Groups

1. Grains (includes bread, cereal, rice, and pasta)
2. Vegetables
3. Fruits
4. Milk (also includes yogurt and cheese)
5. Meat and Beans (also includes poultry, fish, eggs, and nuts)
6. Oils, Fats, and Sweets

french fries _____

corn on the cob _____

pineapple _____

ice cream _____

orange juice _____

grapes _____

hamburger _____

rice and beans _____

corn flakes _____

boiled egg _____

chicken taco _____

yogurt _____

hot cocoa _____

shrimp _____

pizza _____

carrots _____

chili _____

peanut butter sandwich _____

334 SG • Grade 1 • Unit 16 • Lesson 2   Food Sort

Student Guide - page 334 (Answers on p. 31)

Name _____ Date _____

Joni's and Bobbie's Breakfasts

Homework

Joni eats the same breakfast every day. She eats rice puffs, milk, slices of apples, banana bread, and orange juice.

Bobbie eats the same breakfast every day also. She eats a waffle with strawberries, whipped cream, and maple syrup. With it she has bacon and a glass of milk.

Help them find out what food groups their breakfast foods belong to. Write the number(s) of the food group(s) after each food.

Joni's Breakfast	Bobbie's Breakfast
rice puffs _____	waffle _____
milk _____	strawberries _____
slices of apples _____	whipped cream _____
banana bread _____	maple syrup _____
orange juice _____	bacon _____
	milk _____

1. Grains
2. Vegetables
3. Fruits
4. Milk
5. Meat and Beans
6. Oils, Fats, and Sweets

Food Sort   SG • Grade 1 • Unit 16 • Lesson 2 335

Student Guide - page 335 (Answers on p. 32)

At a Glance

Math Facts Strategies and Daily Practice and Problems

DPP item C provides addition math facts practice. Item D is a story problem from the *Student Guide.*

Teaching the Activity (A1)

1. Using the completed *Favorite Foods* Homework Page from Lesson 1, student pairs decide where each of their favorite foods should be placed on the *Food Group Sort 1* Activity Page.
2. Students explore ways to classify fruits and vegetables. If possible, use the book *Eating the Alphabet: Fruits and Vegetables from A to Z* by Lois Ehlert.
3. Student pairs work on the *Food Group Sort 2* Activity Page for practice in classifying foods. Discuss how some of the foods fall into more than one food group.

Homework

Students complete the *Joni's and Bobbie's Breakfasts* Homework Page.

Assessment

Use Assessment Indicator A1 and the *Observational Assessment Record* to document students' abilities to collect and organize data.

Connection

Read and discuss *Eating the Alphabet: Fruits and Vegetables from A to Z* by Lois Ehlert.

Answer Key is on pages 31–32.

Notes:

Student Guide (p. 333)

Food Group Sort 1

Answers will vary depending on the food chosen.

Name _____ Date _____

Food Group Sort 1

You will need your *Favorite Foods* Homework Page. Sort your favorite foods into these six food groups. Write the names of your favorite foods in the boxes below.

Grains (includes bread, cereal, rice, and pasta)	Milk (also includes yogurt and cheese)
Vegetables	**Meat and Beans (also includes poultry, fish, eggs, and nuts)**
Fruits	**Oils, Fats, and Sweets**

Food Sort   SG • Grade 1 • Unit 16 • Lesson 2   333

Student Guide - page 333

Student Guide (p. 334)

Food Group Sort 2

Food	Group(s)
french fries	2, 6
corn on the cob	2
pineapple	3
ice cream	4, 6
orange juice	3
grapes	3
hamburger	5, 6
rice and beans	1, 5
corn flakes	1
boiled egg	5
chicken taco	1, 5
yogurt	4
hot cocoa	4, 6
shrimp	5
pizza	1, 2, 4, 5
carrots	2
chili	2, 5, 6
peanut butter sandwich	1, 5, 6

Name _____ Date _____

Food Group Sort 2

Sort the foods below into these six food groups. Write the number of the group after each food. Some foods are in more than one group.

Food Groups

1. Grains (includes bread, cereal, rice, and pasta)
2. Vegetables
3. Fruits
4. Milk (also includes yogurt and cheese)
5. Meat and Beans (also includes poultry, fish, eggs, and nuts)
6. Oils, Fats, and Sweets

french fries ____   boiled egg ____

corn on the cob ____   chicken taco ____

pineapple ____   yogurt ____

ice cream ____   hot cocoa ____

orange juice ____   shrimp ____

grapes ____   pizza ____

hamburger ____   carrots ____

rice and beans ____   chili ____

corn flakes ____   peanut butter sandwich ____

334   SG • Grade 1 • Unit 16 • Lesson 2   Food Sort

Student Guide - page 334

Student Guide - page 335

Student Guide (p. 335)

Joni's and Bobbie's Breakfasts

Joni's Breakfast

Food	Group(s)
rice puffs	1
milk	4
slices of apples	3
banana bread	1, 3
orange juice	3

Bobbie's Breakfast

Food	Group(s)
waffle	1
strawberries	3
whipped cream	4
maple syrup	6
bacon	5, 6
milk	4

Lesson 3

Healthy Kids

<table>
<tr><td>

Estimated Class Sessions

3

</td><td>

Lesson Overview

In this teacher-guided lab, children collect data on what they eat for one day and then compare their diets to suggested food group amounts. Students graph the data. Children then analyze their personal data and set dietary goals for themselves.

</td></tr>
</table>

Key Content

- Using tallies and symbols to represent numbers.
- Collecting, organizing, graphing, and analyzing data.
- Making and interpreting bar graphs.
- Translating between graphs and real-world events.
- Using data to solve problems.
- Communicating solution strategies verbally and in writing.
- Connecting mathematics and science to real-world situations: conducting a food survey.

Math Facts Strategies

DPP items E, G, and I provide math facts practice. Item F is a problem from the *Student Guide.* Items H and J ask students to group and count objects by twos, fives, and tens.

Homework

Students collect their data for the lab and record it on the *I Ate That!* Homework Pages.

Assessment

1. Students complete the *David's and Cindy's Food* Assessment Pages. Use Assessment Indicators A2 and A3 and the *Observational Assessment Record* to note whether students can make and interpret bar graphs and use data to solve problems.
2. Use Assessment Indicator A4 and the *Observational Assessment Record* to document students' progress with the math facts in Group F. Note students' strategies.
3. Transfer appropriate assessment documentation from the Unit 16 *Observational Assessment Record* to students' *Individual Assessment Record Sheets.*

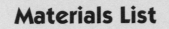

Materials List

Supplies and Copies

Student	Teacher
Supplies for Each Student	**Supplies** • 1 cup of cereal, optional
Copies	**Copies/Transparencies** • 1 transparency of Servings data table (*Student Guide* Page 338) • 1 transparency of *My Pyramid* or classroom poster of food groups and recommended servings (*Unit Resource Guide* Page 42)

All blackline masters including assessment, transparency, and DPP masters are also on the Teacher Resource CD.

Student Books

Home Again (*Student Guide* Page 330)
I Ate That! (*Student Guide* Pages 337–338)
Healthy Kids (*Student Guide* Pages 339–341)
David's and Cindy's Food (*Student Guide* Pages 343–345)

Daily Practice and Problems

DPP items E–J (*Unit Resource Guide* Pages 14–17)

Assessment Tools

Observational Assessment Record (*Unit Resource Guide* Pages 9–10)
Individual Assessment Record Sheet (*Teacher Implementation Guide,* Assessment section)

Daily Practice and Problems

Suggestions for using the DPPs are on pages 39–40.

E. Related Math Facts (URG p. 14)

What other number sentences relate to these four number sentences?

1. $10 + 1 = 11$
2. $10 + 3 = 13$
3. $100 + 10 = 110$
4. $30 + 100 = 130$

F. *Home Again* (URG p. 14)

Turn to page 330 in your *Student Guide*. We are going to read the last page in our story about the boy who liked to solve hard problems.

G. Math Facts 1 (URG p. 15)

1. $9 + 1 =$ $1 + 9 =$
2. $2 + 10 =$ $10 + 2 =$
3. $3 + 9 =$ $9 + 3 =$
4. $4 + 10 =$ $10 + 4 =$

H. More Grouping Beans (URG p. 15)

1. Group the beans by twos and then fill in the blanks for this statement:

   __ groups of __ and __ left over.

2. Now group them by fives and fill in the blanks again.

   __ groups of __ and __ left over.

3. Now group them by tens and fill in the blanks again.

   __ groups of __ and __ left over.

I. Math Facts 2 (URG p. 16)

1. $9 + 1 =$
2. $10 + 4 =$
3. $9 + 2 =$
4. $10 + 1 =$
5. $9 + 4 =$
6. $10 + 2 =$
7. $3 + 10 =$
8. $3 + 9 =$

Explain your strategy for Question 8.

J. Even More Grouping Beans (URG p. 17)

1. Group the beans by twos and then fill in the blanks for this statement:

   __ groups of __ and __ left over.

2. Now group them by fives and fill in the blanks again.

   __ groups of __ and __ left over.

3. Now group them by tens and fill in the blanks again.

   __ groups of __ and __ left over.

Recommended amounts for children 4–8 years old, according to the U.S. Department of Agriculture.

Servings

Food Group	Servings	Serving Size for Selected Food Items
Grains	4–5	• 1 slice of bread, 1 tortilla, or ½ pita • ½ hamburger bun, English muffin, or bagel • ½ cup cooked cereal, rice, or pasta • 1 cup ready-to-eat breakfast cereal
Vegetables	3	• ½ cup cut-up raw or cooked vegetables • ½ cup vegetable juice • 1 cup leafy raw vegetables, such as lettuce, greens, or spinach
Fruits	3	• a whole fruit, such as medium apple, banana, or orange • ½ cup of juice • ½ grapefruit • ½ cup of berries • ½ cup canned fruit • ¼ cup dried fruit
Milk	2	• 1 cup milk • 1 cup yogurt • 1½ ounces natural cheese • 2 ounces processed cheese
Meat and Beans	3–4	• 1 ounce of lean meat, poultry, or fish • ½ ounce nuts or seeds • 1 egg or ¼ cup tofu • 1 tablespoon peanut butter • ½ cup cooked beans
Oils	4 tsp.* *Most Americans get enough oil in the food they eat.	These foods are mostly oil: • soft margarine • salad dressing • mayonnaise • vegetable oil These foods contain oil: • nuts • peanut butter • avocados • fish
Extra Fats and Sweets	Limit your amount	• candy bar • butter, stick margarine • ice cream • bacon, fat from meat • cakes, cookies • soda, fruit drinks

Copyright © Kendall/Hunt Publishing Company

Student Guide - page 338

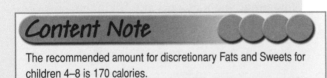

Content Note

The recommended amount for discretionary Fats and Sweets for children 4–8 is 170 calories.

Before the Lab

Lesson 1, the Adventure Book *The Martians,* provides a setting for this investigation. Your class should complete Lesson 2 *Food Sort* before beginning this lab so that children understand how to classify food items into the six food groups. Your students' performance on the *Joni's and Bobbie's Breakfasts* Homework Page can help you determine whether children need more practice before proceeding.

Teaching the Lab

In this lab, students record the number of servings they eat in each food group during the course of one day. Then they are introduced to the government daily intake suggestions and graph their data to investigate how their daily diet compares.

Part 1 Launching the Investigation

Remind students of the Adventure Book *The Martians* in which Dopp and Zorka are interested in studying what children eat. Tell students they are going to help Dopp and Zorka by collecting data about what each student eats in one day.

Discuss what students ate yesterday. Use prompts like the following:

* *Think of all the food you ate yesterday. When did you eat each food?*

* *Do you think you can really remember everything you ate yesterday?*

* *How can we solve this problem?*

Children will probably decide that trying to think of everything they ate yesterday is difficult and unreliable. Discuss with students how to keep track of the foods they eat in the course of a day. They may suggest that after every meal, they record what they have eaten.

Then, ask:

* *What is a good way of categorizing the food so that it can be recorded?*

Students may recall the last lesson, *Food Sort.* They may suggest classifying the foods they have eaten in one day into six food groups.

Finally, discuss how to record the amount of each type of food that is eaten. Display a transparency of the Servings data table on the *I Ate That!* Homework Pages and discuss the meaning of one serving. You may wish to show students one serving of cereal. Ask:

* *Who eats cereal for breakfast? Do you think you eat one serving, two servings, or more?*

Similar examples will help students estimate the number of servings of each type of food they eat during the time the data is collected.

Describe and model how students can use the *I Ate That!* Homework Pages to keep a 24-hour record of the number of servings eaten from each food group during each meal (or snack) of the day. Discuss what constitutes one serving for each food listed in the data table, and tell children that their parents will help them use this information at home. You may need to explain how to use tallies to record the number of servings eaten. Each tally mark represents one serving.

Remind children of the peanut butter sandwich and the hamburger on the *Food Group Sort 2* Activity Page from Lesson 2. These foods are combination foods and provide an opportunity for some detective work. Suggest that if they have trouble with a mixed food, they can simply tally the major food(s) that can be seen easily.

Have the class decide when to begin the 24-hour data collection. Tell children to record this date in the parent note on their copies of the *I Ate That!* Homework Pages. By completing the *I Ate That!* Homework Pages, students are collecting their data for the lab. These pages should be assigned after this first day of the lab.

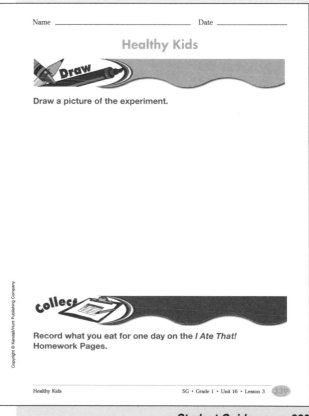

TIMS Tip

A Saturday or Sunday might be more convenient than a weekday since children would not need to bring their data tables to and from school. For practice, you may wish to tally what students eat for lunch the first day of the lab.

TIMS Tip

Be sure children understand that their data collection begins when they get up in the morning and ends when they go to bed at night.

Part 2 Drawing the Picture
After the initial discussion, children draw pictures on the *Healthy Kids* Lab Pages to organize their thoughts about the lab. They should know that they are recording data about the foods they eat on a given date and that they will compare their intake to a suggested, healthy diet.

Children's drawings should show that they are sorting foods into groups and recording the number of servings. The date should also be recorded on their pictures.

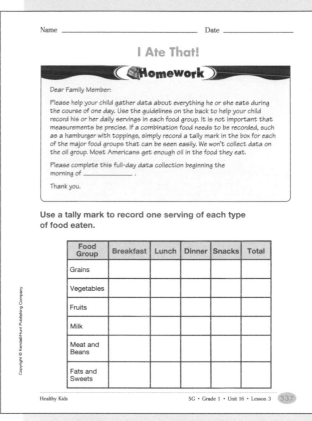

Student Guide - page 337 (Answers on p. 43)

Student Guide - page 339

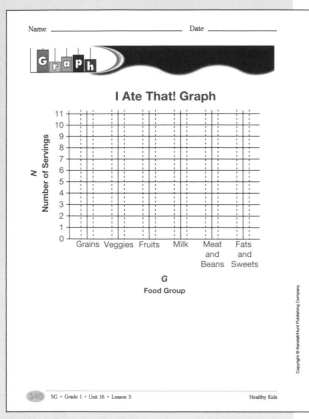

Name _____ Date _____

I Ate That! Graph

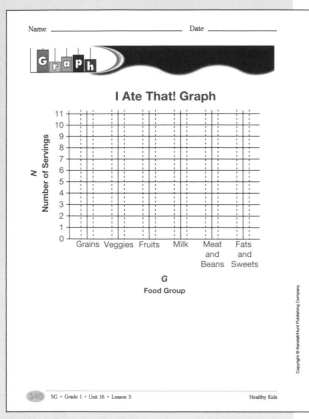

Student Guide - page 340

Part 3   Collecting and Graphing the Data

When children return with their completed data tables, introduce them to the U.S. Department of Agriculture's recommendation for appropriate daily food intake by displaying the *My Pyramid* Transparency Master or by featuring a classroom food groups poster. Explain that many scientists study healthy diets. This food pyramid was created to show the amount of each food group that should be eaten to help people stay healthy.

If children have not already totaled their own data for each food group at home, they should do so now. Then, they should transfer their data to the I Ate That! graph provided on the lab pages.

Part 4   Exploring the Data

A healthy diet is based on eating a variety of foods and choosing an appropriate proportion of one's intake from suitable food groups. The food pyramid provides one representation of the proportions. The graph is another way to show the same proportions.

The Explore section of the lab pages gives children the opportunity to think about how their daily diet compares with the recommended amounts. Ask questions similar to the following:

- *Did you eat more or fewer servings of milk than was suggested?*
- *What should you eat more of?*
- *What should you eat less of?*

Encourage students to use the USDA recommended amounts as they make their Healthier Kids graph of a better diet in *Question 2.*

To conclude the lab, you can ask:

- *If the Martians looked at your I Ate That! Graph, would they think you are eating a healthy, balanced diet?*

Children can share their ideas with each other.

Journal Prompt

Use your graph to help you tell the story of your food choices. Write a letter to the Martians telling them about your diet. Do you need to change anything?

Math Facts Strategies

DPP item E explores related addition and subtraction facts. DPP items G and I provide addition math facts practice.

Homework and Practice

- The *I Ate That!* Homework Pages are the data collection for this lab and should be assigned after the first day of the lab.
- Assign DPP items F, H, and J. Item F is a story problem from the *Student Guide.* Items H and J provide practice with grouping and counting beans with twos, fives, and tens and counting leftovers.

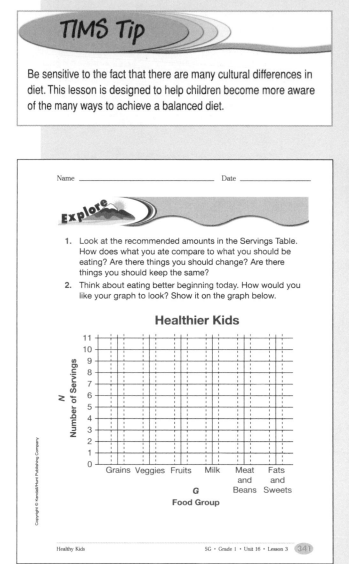

Name _____ Date _____

Explore

1. Look at the recommended amounts in the Servings Table. How does what you ate compare to what you should be eating? Are there things you should change? Are there things you should keep the same?
2. Think about eating better beginning today. How would you like your graph to look? Show it on the graph below.

Healthier Kids

Student Guide - page 341 (Answers on p. 43)

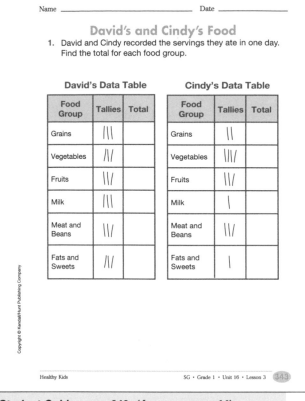

Name _____ Date _____

David's and Cindy's Food

1. David and Cindy recorded the servings they ate in one day. Find the total for each food group.

David's Data Table

Food Group	Tallies	Total
Grains	|||	
Vegetables	/|/	
Fruits	||/	
Milk	|||	
Meat and Beans	||/	
Fats and Sweets	/|/	

Cindy's Data Table

Food Group	Tallies	Total
Grains	||	
Vegetables	|||/	
Fruits	||/	
Milk	|	
Meat and Beans	||/	
Fats and Sweets	|	

Copyright © Kendall/Hunt Publishing Company

Healthy Kids   SG • Grade 1 • Unit 16 • Lesson 3   343

Student Guide - page 343 *(Answers on p. 44)*

Assessment

- Use *David's and Cindy's Food* Assessment Pages to assess whether children can make and interpret bar graphs and solve problems using data. Record students' progress on the *Observational Assessment Record*.

- *Questions 1–2* in the Explore section on the *Healthy Kids* Lab Pages and children's responses to the Journal Prompt can be used to assess whether children can interpret data and use it to plan a healthy diet.

- Use DPP item I to assess students' progress with the addition math facts in Group F. Using ten or counting on are appropriate strategies for these facts. Document students' progress on the *Observational Assessment Record.* Note which strategies students use.

- Transfer appropriate assessment documentation from the Unit 16 *Observational Assessment Record* to students' *Individual Assessment Record Sheets.*

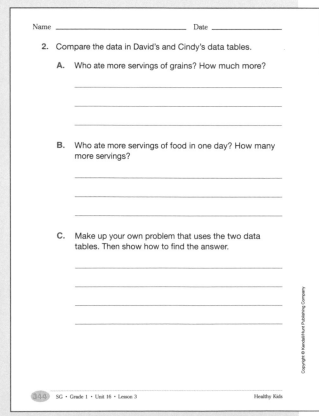

Name _____ Date _____

2. Compare the data in David's and Cindy's data tables.

   A. Who ate more servings of grains? How much more?

   _____

   _____

   _____

   B. Who ate more servings of food in one day? How many more servings?

   _____

   _____

   _____

   C. Make up your own problem that uses the two data tables. Then show how to find the answer.

   _____

   _____

   _____

   _____

344   SG • Grade 1 • Unit 16 • Lesson 3   Healthy Kids

Student Guide - page 344 *(Answers on p. 44)*

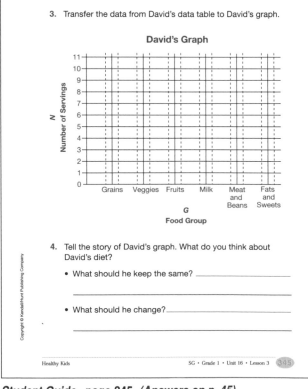

Name _____ Date _____

3. Transfer the data from David's data table to David's graph.

David's Graph

Number of Servings (N) — vertical axis marked 0 through 11

Food Group (G) — horizontal axis: Grains, Veggies, Fruits, Milk, Meat and Beans, Fats and Sweets

4. Tell the story of David's graph. What do you think about David's diet?

   • What should he keep the same? _____

   _____

   • What should he change? _____

   _____

Healthy Kids   SG • Grade 1 • Unit 16 • Lesson 3   345

Student Guide - page 345 *(Answers on p. 45)*

Estimated Class Sessions

3

At a Glance

Math Facts Strategies and Daily Practice and Problems

DPP items E, G, and I provide math facts practice. Item F is a problem from the *Student Guide.* Items H and J ask students to group and count objects by twos, fives, and tens.

Part 1. Launching the Investigation

1. Remind students of *The Martians* Adventure Book story. Discuss what students eat.
2. Display a transparency of the Servings data table on the *I Ate That!* Homework Pages and discuss the meaning of one serving.
3. Discuss how to record the amount of each type of food eaten.
4. The class decides when to begin the 24-hour data collection. Students record this date in the parent note on the *I Ate That!* Homework Pages.

Part 2. Drawing the Picture

Children draw pictures on the *Healthy Kids* Lab Pages. Their drawings should include the date and show that they are putting foods into groups and recording the number of servings.

Part 3. Collecting and Graphing the Data (A1) (A2)

1. Introduce students to the USDA's *My Pyramid* using a transparency.
2. Students total the day's tallies for each food group.
3. Students transfer their data to the I Ate That! graph on the *Healthy Kids* Lab Pages.

Part 4. Exploring the Data (A2) (A3)

1. Students complete the Explore questions on the *Healthy Kids* Lab Pages.
2. Students set dietary goals for themselves by completing the Healthier Kids graph.
3. Ask: *"If the Martians saw your graph, would they think you eat a healthy diet?"*

Homework

Students collect their data for the lab and record it on the *I Ate That!* Homework Pages.

Assessment

1. Students complete the *David's and Cindy's Food* Assessment Pages. Use Assessment Indicators A2 and A3 and the *Observational Assessment Record* to note whether students can make and interpret bar graphs and use data to solve problems.
2. Use Assessment Indicator A4 and the *Observational Assessment Record* to document students' progress with the math facts in Group F. Note students' strategies.
3. Transfer appropriate assessment documentation from the Unit 16 *Observational Assessment Record* to students' *Individual Assessment Record Sheets.*

Answer Key is on pages 43–45.

Notes:

My Pyramid

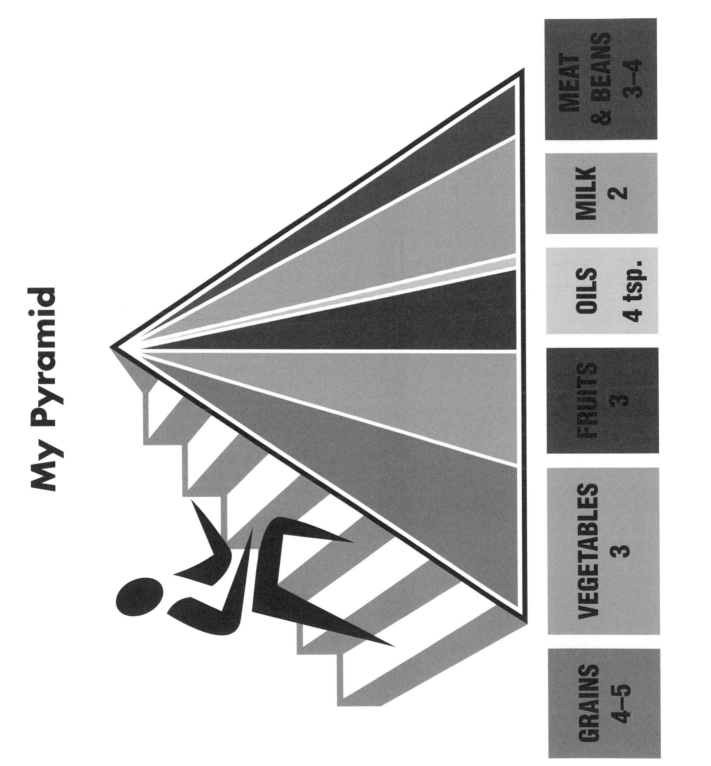

GRAINS
4–5

VEGETABLES
3

FRUITS
3

OILS
4 tsp.

MILK
2

MEAT
& BEANS
3–4

Transparency Master

Student Guide (p. 337)

I Ate That!

Answers will vary depending upon the foods eaten.

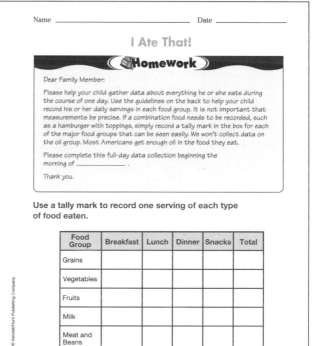

Student Guide (p. 341)

Healthy Kids

Pictures, graphs, and answers to *Questions 1–2* will vary depending upon data collected.

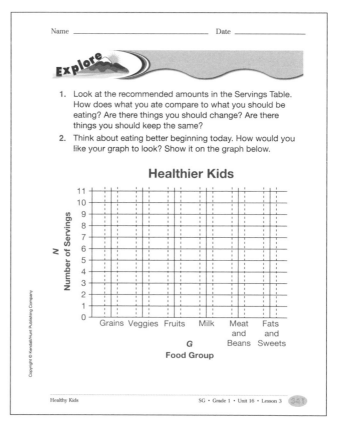

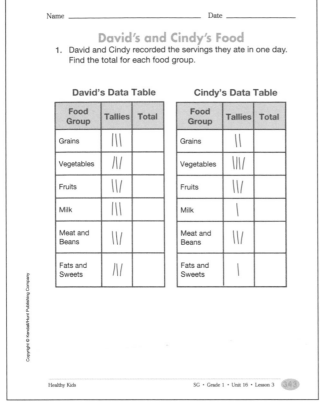

Student Guide - page 343

Student Guide (p. 343)

David's and Cindy's Food

1.   David's Data Table

Food Group	Tallies	Total
Grains	|||	3
Vegetables	|||	3
Fruits	|||	3
Milk	|||	3
Meat and Beans	|||	3
Fats/Sweets	|||	3

Student Guide (p. 344)

David's and Cindy's Food

Cindy's Data Table

Food Group	Tallies	Total
Grains	||	2
Vegetables	||||	4
Fruits	|||	3
Milk	|	1
Meat and Beans	|||	3
Fats/Sweets	|	1

2. **A.** David ate one serving more of Grains than Cindy.

   B. David ate 4 more servings of food than Cindy in one day.

   C. Problems will vary.

Student Guide - page 344

Student Guide (p. 345)

David's and Cindy's Food

3.

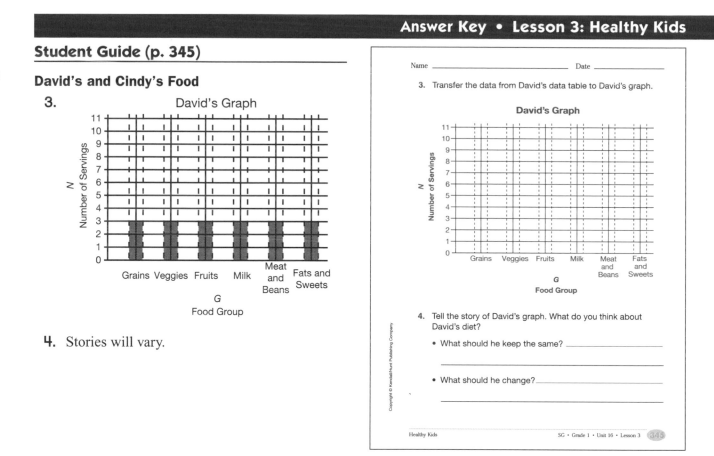

4. Stories will vary.

Glossary

This glossary provides definitions of key vocabulary terms in the Grade 1 lessons. Locations of key vocabulary terms in the curriculum are included with each definition. Components Key: URG = *Unit Resource Guide* and SG = *Student Guide.*

A

Approximate (URG Unit 12)
1. (adjective) a number that is close to the desired number
2. (verb) to estimate

Area (URG Unit 10; SG Unit 12)
The amount of space that a shape covers. Area is measured in square units.

B

C

Capacity (URG Unit 9)
1. The volume of the inside of a container.
2. The largest volume a container can hold.

Circle (URG Unit 2)
A curve that is made up of all the points that are the same distance from one point, the center.

Circumference (URG Unit 15)
The distance around a circle.

Coordinates (URG Unit 19)
(In the plane) Two numbers that specify the location of a point on a flat surface relative to a reference point called the origin. The two numbers are the distances from the point to two perpendicular lines called axes.

Counting All (URG Unit 1)
A strategy for adding in which students start at one and count until the total is reached.

Counting Back (URG Unit 8)
A method of subtraction that involves counting from the larger number to the smaller one. For example, to find 8 − 5 the student counts 7, 6, 5 which is 3 less.

Counting On (URG Unit 1 & Unit 4)
A strategy for adding two numbers in which students start with one of the numbers and then count until the total is reached. For example, to count 6 + 3, begin with 6 and count three more, 7, 8, 9.

Counting Up (URG Unit 8)
A method of subtraction that involves counting from the smaller number to the larger one. For example, to find 8 − 5 the student counts 6, 7, 8 which is 3 more.

Cube (URG Unit 12 & Unit 15)
A solid with six congruent square faces.

Cubic Units (URG Unit 12)
A unit for measuring volume— a cube that measures one unit along each edge. For example, cubic centimeters and cubic inches.

cubic centimeter

Cylinder (URG Unit 15)
A three-dimensional figure with two parallel congruent circles as bases (top and bottom) and a curved side that is the union of parallel lines connecting corresponding points on the circles.

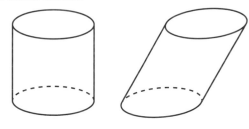

D

Data Table (URG Unit 3)
A tool for recording and organizing data on paper or on a computer.

Name	Age

Division by Measuring Out (URG Unit 14)
A type of division problem in which the number in each group is known and the unknown is the number of groups. For example, twenty students are divided into teams of four students each. How many teams are there? (20 students ÷ 4 students per team = 5 teams) This type of division is also known as measurement division.

Division by Sharing (URG Unit 14)
A type of division problem in which the number of groups is known and the unknown is the number in each group. For example, twenty students are divided into five teams. How many students are on each team? (20 students ÷ 5 teams = 4 students per team) This type of division is also known as partitive division.

E

Edge (URG Unit 15)
A line segment where two faces of a three-dimensional figure meet.

Equivalent Fractions (URG Unit 18)
Two fractions are equivalent if they represent the same part of the whole. For example, if a class has 8 boys and 8 girls, we can say $\frac{8}{16}$ of the students are girls or $\frac{1}{2}$ of the students are girls.

Even Number (URG Unit 4 & Unit 13)
Numbers that are doubles. The numbers 0, 2, 4, 6, 8, 10, etc. are even. The number 28 is even because it is 14 + 14.

F

Face (URG Unit 12 & Unit 15)
A flat side of a three-dimensional figure.

Fixed Variables (URG Unit 2, Unit 6 & Unit 11)
Variables in an experiment that are held constant or not changed. These variables are often called controlled variables.

G

H

Hexagon (URG Unit 2)
A six-sided polygon.

I

J

K

L

Length (URG Unit 6 & Unit 10)
1. The distance along a line or curve from one point to another. Distance can be measured with a ruler or tape measure.
2. The distance from one "end" to another of a two- or three-dimensional figure. For example, the length of a rectangle usually refers to the length of the longer side.

Line
A set of points that form a straight path extending infinitely in two directions.

Line Symmetry (URG Unit 7 & Unit 18)
A figure has line symmetry if it can be folded along a line so that the two halves match exactly.

Line of Symmetry (URG Unit 7 & Unit 18)
A line such that if a figure is folded along the line, then one half of the figure matches the other.

M

Making a Ten (URG Unit 13)
A strategy for adding and subtracting that takes advantage of students' knowledge of partitions of ten. For example, a student might find 8 + 4 by breaking the 4 into 2 + 2 and then using a knowledge of sums that add to ten.

$$8 + 4 =$$
$$8 + 2 + 2 =$$
$$10 + 2 = 12$$

Median (URG Unit 6 & Unit 9)
The number "in the middle" of a set of data. If there is an odd number of data, it is the number in the middle when the numbers are arranged in order. So the median of {1, 2, 14, 15, 28, 29, 30} is 15. If there is an even number of data, it is the number halfway between the two middle numbers. The median of {1, 2, 14, 15, 28, 29} is $14\frac{1}{2}$.

Mr. Origin (URG Unit 19)
A plastic figure used to help childen learn about direction and distance.

N

Near Double (URG Unit 13)
A derived addition or subtraction fact found by using doubles. For example, 3 + 4 = 7 follows from the fact that 3 + 3 = 6.

Number Sentence (URG Unit 3 & Unit 4)
A number sentence uses numbers and symbols instead of words to describe a problem. For example, a number sentence for the problem "5 birds landed on a branch. Two more birds also landed on the branch. How many birds are on the branch?" is 5 + 2 = 7.

O

Odd Number (URG Unit 4)
A number that is not even. The odd numbers are 1, 3, 5, 7, 9, and so on.

Origin (URG Unit 19)
A reference point for a coordinate system. If the coordinate system is a line, we can determine the location of an object on the line by the number of units it is to the right or the left of the origin.

P

Part (URG Unit 4)
One of the addends in part-part-whole addition problems.

Pattern Unit (URG Unit 7)
The portion of a pattern that is repeated. For example, AAB is the pattern unit in the pattern AABAABAAB.

Perimeter (URG Unit 6; SG Unit 12)
The distance around a two-dimensional shape.

Polygon
A closed, connected plane figure consisting of line segments, with exactly two segments meeting at each end point.

Polygons

Not Polygons

Prediction (URG Unit 5)
Using a sample to predict what is likely to occur in the population.

Prism (URG Unit 15)
A solid that has two congruent and parallel bases. The remaining faces (sides) are parallelograms. A rectangular prism has bases that are rectangles. A box is a common object that is shaped like a rectangular prism.

Q

Quadrilateral
A polygon with four sides.

R

Rectangle (URG Unit 2)
A quadrilateral with four right angles.

Rhombus (URG Unit 2)
A quadrilateral with four sides of equal length.

Rotational Symmetry (URG Unit 7)
A figure has rotational (or turn) symmetry if there is a point on the figure and a rotation of less than 360° about that point so that it "fits" on itself. For example, a square has a turn symmetry of $\frac{1}{4}$ turn (or 90°) about its center.

S

Sample (URG Unit 5)
Some of the items from a whole group.

Sphere (URG Unit 15)
A three-dimensional figure that is made up of points that are the same distance from one point, the center. A basketball is a common object shaped like a sphere.

Square (URG Unit 2)
A polygon with four equal sides and four right angles.

Symmetry (URG Unit 18)
(See Line Symmetry, Line of Symmetry, and Rotational Symmetry.)

T

Three-dimensional Shapes (URG Unit 15)
A figure in space that has length, width, and height.

TIMS Laboratory Method (URG Unit 5)
A method that students use to organize experiments and investigations. It involves four components: draw, collect, graph, and explore. It is a way to help students learn about the scientific method. TIMS is an acronym for Teaching Integrated Mathematics and Science.

Trapezoid (URG Unit 2)
A quadrilateral with exactly one pair of parallel sides.

Trial (URG Unit 6)
One attempt in an experiment.

Triangle (URG Unit 2)
A polygon with three sides.

Turn Symmetry
(See Rotational Symmetry.)

U

Using Doubles (URG Unit 13)
A strategy for adding and subtracting which uses derived facts from known doubles. For example, students use 7 + 7 = 14 to find that 7 + 8 is one more or 15.

Using Ten (URG Unit 13)
A strategy for adding which uses reasoning from known facts. For example, students use 3 + 7 = 10 to find that 4 + 7 is one more or 11.

V

Variable (URG Unit 2 & Unit 11)
A variable is something that varies or changes in an experiment.

Volume (URG Unit 9 & Unit 12;
  SG Unit 12)
1. The amount of space an object takes up.
2. The amount of space inside a container.

W

Whole (URG Unit 4)
The sum in part-part-whole addition problems.

X

Y

Z